PowerKids Readers:
My World of Science™

Sounds in My World

Los sonidos en mi mundo

Joanne Randolph

Traducción al español: María Cristina Brusca

The Rosen Publishing Group's
PowerKids Press™ & **Editorial Buenas Letras**™

For Linda Lou and Lucas

Published in 2006 by The Rosen Publishing Group, Inc.
29 East 21st Street, New York, NY 10010

First Edition

Photo Credits: Cover and p. 21(boy) © Ariel Skelley/Corbis; Cover and p. 17 (bird) © Niall Bevie/Corbis; Cover (dog) © Tim Davis/Corbis; p. 5 © Craig Tuttle/Corbis; p. 7 © Bill Deering/Getty Images; pp. 9, 13, 19, 22 (ambulance), (siren) © Royalty-Free/Corbis; pp. 11, 22 (laugh) © Rolf Bruderer/Corbis; p. 15 © Mel Yates/Getty Images; p. 22 (drum) © Robert Holmgren/Getty Images.

Library of Congress Cataloging-in-Publication Data

Randolph, Joanne.
[Sounds in my world. Spanish & English]
Sounds in my world = Los sonidos en mi mundo / Joanne Randolph ; traducción al español, María Cristina Brusca.— 1st ed.
p. cm. — (My world of science)
Includes bibliographical references and index. ISBN 1-4042-3318-0 (lib. bdg.)
1. Sound—Juvenile literature. I. Title: Sonidos en mi mundo. II. Title.
QC225.5.R3618 2006
534—dc22
2005007164

Manufactured in the United States of America

Contents

Contenido

Sounds are what we call the things we can hear with our ears. We hear sounds every day. We listen to waves crash at the beach. We hear cars pass by on the street.

Llamamos sonido a aquello que podemos escuchar con nuestros oídos. Todos los días oímos sonidos. Escuchamos cómo rompen las olas en la playa. Oímos a los autos cuando pasan por la calle.

Sound cannot be seen. Barking dogs make sound. All sound is made up of waves of air. These waves move. Our ears hear the waves as the different sounds things make.

Los sonidos no se pueden ver. Al ladrar, los perros producen sonidos. Todos los sonidos están formados por ondas de aire. Estas ondas se mueven. Nuestros oídos oyen las ondas cuando las cosas producen los diferentes sonidos.

Some sounds are soft. Wind blowing through the leaves can be soft. A whisper is soft. A cat's footsteps sound soft, too. Can you think of other soft sounds?

Algunos sonidos son bajos. Cuando el viento sopla las hojas, el sonido puede ser bajo. Un murmullo es bajo. El sonido de los pasos de un gato también es bajo. ¿Puedes pensar en otros sonidos bajos?

Some sounds are loud. A marching band makes a loud sound. A laugh can be loud, too. Thunder can sometimes be loud. What else makes a loud sound?

Algunos sonidos son altos. Una banda de música produce un sonido alto. La risa también puede ser alta. A veces los truenos pueden ser altos. ¿Qué otras cosas producen sonidos altos?

Some loud sounds tell us that something is wrong. The siren on an ambulance makes this kind of sound. A fire alarm makes this kind of sound, too.

Algunos sonidos altos nos avisan cuando hay algún peligro. La sirena de una ambulancia produce esa clase de sonido. Una alarma de incendio hace también esa clase de sonido.

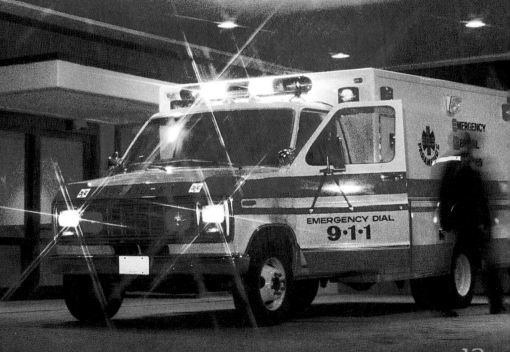

AMBULANCE

EMERGENCY DIAL
9·1·1

13

Sounds can be low. A low sound is deep and rumbling. The moo of a cow is a low sound. A drum makes a low sound, too. These sounds can be loud or soft.

Los sonidos pueden ser graves. Un sonido grave es profundo y retumbante. El mugido de una vaca es un sonido grave. Un tambor también hace sonidos graves. Estos sonidos pueden ser altos o bajos.

Some sounds are high. They can sound sharp. A cat's meow is a high sound. A bird's call is a high sound, too. Think of other sounds that are high.

Algunos sonidos son agudos. Estos sonidos pueden ser muy intensos. El maullido de un gato es un sonido agudo. El canto de un pájaro es un sonido agudo. Piensa en otros sonidos que sean agudos.

When we talk to each other our voices are making sounds. We form the sounds into different words. This is how we are able to talk and share news with each other.

Cuando platicamos, nuestras voces están haciendo sonidos. Con los sonidos formamos las palabras. De esa forma podemos hablar y compartir nuestras novedades.

Sounds are everywhere in our world. Think about all the different sounds you hear each day. What are some of the sounds that could be made by things in this picture?

Hay sonidos en todas partes de nuestro mundo. Piensa acerca de todos los sonidos que escuchas cada día. ¿Cuáles son algunos de los sonidos que podrían hacer las cosas que hay en esta foto?

21

Words to Know
Palabras que debes saber

ambulance
ambulancia

drum
tambor

laugh
risa

siren
sirena

Here are more books to read about sounds:
Otros libros que puedes leer sobre los sonidos:

In English/En inglés
All About Sound (Rookie Read-About Science)
by Lisa Trumbauer
Children's Press

In Spanish/En Español
Ciencia Divertida, Sonido y Música
by Barbara Taylor
Mega Ediciones

Web Sites/En Internet
Due to the changing nature of Internet links, PowerKids Press and Editorial Buenas Letras have developed an online list of Web sites related to the subject of this book. This site is updated regularly. Please use this link to access the list:

www.powerkidslinks.com/mws/sounds/

Index

A
ambulance, 12

C
cars, 4

D
dogs, 6
drum, 14

H
high sounds, 16

L
low sounds, 14

T
talk, 18
thunder, 10

Índice

A
ambulancia, 12
autos, 4

H
hablar, 18

P
perros, 6

S
sonidos agudos, 16
sonidos graves, 14

T
tambor, 14
trueno, 10

Word Count: 277

Número de palabras: 290

Note to Librarians, Teachers, and Parents

PowerKids Readers are specially designed to help emergent and beginning readers build their skills in reading for information. Sentences are short and simple, employing a basic vocabulary of sight words, simple vocabulary, and basic concepts, as well as new words that describe objects or processes that relate to the topic. Large type, clean design, and stunning photographs corresponding directly to the text all help children to decipher meaning. Features such as a contents page, picture glossary, and index introduce children to the basic elements of a book, which they will encounter in their future reading experiences.